For Ree, Tamara and Ethan, with love – V. B.
To Luba – K. W–M.

Text copyright © Valerie Bloom 2021
Illustrations copyright © Ken Wilson-Max 2021
Designed by Arianna Osti
First published in Great Britain and in the USA in 2021 by
Otter-Barry Books, Little Orchard, Burley Gate,
Herefordshire, HR1 3QS
www.otterbarrybooks.com

FSC
www.fsc.org
MIX
Paper from
responsible sources
FSC® C018072

ISBN 978-1-91307-467-8

Illustrated with pencil and digital ink

Set in Sabon

Printed in Great Britain

9 8 7 6 5 4 3

STARS WITH FLAMING TAILS

by Valerie Bloom

Illustrated by
Ken Wilson-Max

Otter-Barry BOOKS

CONTENTS

FAMILY AND FRIENDS

FUN WITH FORMS

OUR WORLD

ANIMALS

UNBELIEVABLE?

FAMILY AND FRIENDS

WELCOME

And on the eighth day they knew for certain
That she had come to stay,
So they touched her lips,
And stroked sugar on her palm,
With ginger for health and oil for calm,
Water for cleansing and washing out strife,
Salt for happiness, cola nut for long life,

And so she tasted the world.

Then the sound of her name
Gave speech to the drums,
Made poets of her kinsmen.

"Now," they said,
"Like the rooster whose feet have passed
Through the fire,
You will stay with us."

The feasting and dancing would last
All night,
But she would dream of whispers from the sea.

And when a wrinkled face unwrapped empty gums
Above her,
Startling her into whimpers,
Her mother's voice was the sea,
Breaking in gentle waves over her.

Bya bya mi baby
Baby want to sleepy
Sleepy, sleepy,
Baby want to sleep.

And the sea whispered,
"Welcome, Chinelo. Welcome."

YOU ARE

You are the silver in the moonlight
The waves kissing the beach
The nectar in the mango
The sweetness in the peach.

You are the perfume of the jasmine
Winter's virgin snow
The softness of a velvet cushion
A sunset's golden glow.

You're the contented purr of the kitten
The orange groves of Spain
The silence of soft midnight
And a favourite tune's refrain.

Flowers bloom in winter
Warm sunlight bathes the ground
And birdsong fills the neighbourhood
Whenever you're around.

MUM SAYS SHE LOVES ME

Mum says she loves me
And I believe her,
Dad says he loves me
And he's not a deceiver,
They say that they'll always
Love me forever.
I only wish
They could love me together.

NOTHING TO DO

There are dishes in the sink
And they're begging to be washed,
There's the mess to be cleaned up
From that banana you just squashed.

Come with me for a minute,
Let me show you to your room,
It is gasping for a visit
From the dustpan and the broom.

It appears that all your bedclothes
Have been fighting with your bed,
And that plate of old spaghetti
I am sure has long been dead.

There's a curtain of old cobwebs
Stretched across your bedroom wall,
And muddy wellies do not add
To the decor in the hall.

Did you say that you've gone out
And got yourself a maid?
Then who is going to clear up
That spilt cake and orangeade?

Come along, I'll introduce you
To someone you ought to meet,
This is Lady Vacuum Cleaner,
She makes homes tidy and neat.

So you've finished all your homework
And packed your school bag, I suppose?
There are a million things to do
Right underneath your nose.

I wonder why Mum
Has to get in such a stew
When I tell her that I'm bored
And there's nothing here to do.

ADAM HAD AN ACCiDENT

When Adam had an accident
(he fell and hurt his arm),
Bernie brought a bottle,
Try some of this lemon balm.
Carol said, No, that won't do,
he needs some camomile.
That arm will need the doctor,
Dennis said with a wry smile.
Ellie said, Evening primrose
on the cut will give some ease.
Freddy waved a fennel bulb,
saying, Can you let him try this, please?
Grace held aloft some ginger root.
This will kill the germs.
Harry said, Heart's ease is best,
in no uncertain terms.
Ian brought an iris, saying,
I think that this will do.
Janet picked some juniper berries.
Put these in his shoe.
Karen said, My mum's kale chips,
They are the perfect mender.
I know what will revive him best,
Said Lionel, that's lavender.
Mint, said Marcy, Neem, said Neil,
Raw onions, said young Orville.
Plantain's good for cuts, said Paul,
but perhaps he needs a large pill.

Quinine, said Quentin, Rosemary, said Rose,
A saffron salad, said Sally.
Tansy's best, said Tilly-Ann,
I saw that on the telly.
Ulmus Fulvus, said Umberto.
They all cried, What's that?
Not really sure, but I saw
Dad use it on the cat.
The very best is vervain,
or valerian, said Vance.
Wendy frowned and looked around.
Is there wormwood by any chance?
Xylopia, said Xara,
who was taking Latin at school,
Ylang-ylang on his head, said Yuan,
will soothe and keep him cool.
Zingiber, said Zavier.
That's just ginger, someone said.

Meanwhile Adam left them arguing
and hurried home to bed!

BEST FRIENDS

If you were a soldier and I were your enemy
I wouldn't fight you
If you were a deer and I were a lion
I wouldn't bite you

If you were a fish and I were a net
I wouldn't catch you
If you were a bone and I were a dog
I wouldn't snatch you

If you were a fly and I were a swatter
I wouldn't kill you
If you were water and I were a carrier
I wouldn't spill you

If you were a cup I'd be a saucer
And let you rest on me
And we will be best friends from now
Until eternity.

WHEN MUMMY COMBS MY HAIR

She tugs and pulls and twists and yanks,
My hair sticks to the comb in hanks,

She yanks and tugs and pulls and twists,
My hair falls to the floor in bits,

She twists and yanks and tugs and pulls,
Hair's on the floor in large handfuls,

She pulls and twists and yanks and tugs,
Looks at my bald head, calmly shrugs.

She thinks that I won't mind at all,
Because I'm just a little doll.

PANCAKES

My brother made some pancakes
Last night for our tea,
But when we'd eaten the whole lot
We were all still hungry.
We'd each had half a pancake
So we looked around for more,
And we found them on the ceiling
And on the kitchen floor.

WE DON'T LAUGH WHEN GRANDAD SINGS

When Grandad sings he shuts his eyes,
Screws up his face, points to the skies.
His mouth and nostrils open wide,
His hips start moving side to side.
He does the most outrageous things,
But we don't laugh when Grandad sings.

When Grandad sings he stamps the floor,
He slaps his hands against the door
As if he's playing a big bass drum,
He jerks his shoulders, shakes his bum.
He does the most outrageous things,
But we don't laugh when Grandad sings.

When Grandad sings the whole house shakes,
The plates all rattle, the baby wakes,
The cat flies yowling up the stairs,
Grandma says, "Quick, cover your ears!"
He does the most outrageous things,
But we don't laugh when Grandad sings.

Grandad's feelings would be hurt
If we should greet his songs with mirth,
He'd go quiet, he'd look dejected
And all of us would be affected.
He does the most outrageous things,
But we don't laugh when Grandad sings.

Hide and Seek

They can't see me way up here,
they don't know where I am,
they're looking for me inside the house,
I can hear the back door slam.

They think I'm in my bedroom,
or in the cellar I bet,
they've been looking for me for hours now
and they haven't found me yet.

They'll be looking for me in the kitchen now,
in the cupboards, under the sink,
they'll be looking in the bathroom
and behind the telly, I think.

Now that they've searched all the rooms,
they'll be wondering where I could be,
none of them will ever guess
I'm hiding in this tree.

They've found Riley and Zara,
but I am much too clever.
Wait! What if they never find me
and I have to stay up here forever!

What if they have all gone home
and I'm stuck here till next year?
What if I can't get down?
Hey, guys! Look! I'm up here!

CONTRARY CARL

If I say it's a train,
he will say it's a bus,
I say my name's Arlan,
he says, "No, it's Gus."
I said, "Here's a stone."
He said, "It's a bed."
I said, "Duck!" He said, "Goose!"
Now he's a lump on his head.

TiME LiKE A BABY

When I'm hungry,
Lunch an hour away,
Time creeps like a baby,
Lengthening the day.

When I'm waiting for dinner
Time doesn't hurry at all,
But goes like a baby
Learning to crawl.

Yet when I'm having fun
With my mates out at play,
Time is an arrow
Speeding away.

THROUGH MY WiNDOW

There's food on the table, a family sits down to eat,
there are crisp roast potatoes, vegetables and meat,
afterwards there's ice-cream the mother's made as a
    treat.
That's what I see through my window.

The door opens and the family goes outside,
the children play on the swings and the slide,
the parents watch them, with love and with pride.
That's what I see through my window.

The father dandles the baby on his knee,
the two boys are playing Monopoly,
the mother and daughter are watching TV.
That's what I see through my window.

The family sits in a circle on the floor,
the father's reading a story they might have heard
    before,
the little one is sleeping, you can hear his gentle
    snore.
That's what I see through my window.

The family's well fed, the baby's not screaming,
it's not cold and damp, the walls are not streaming.
My father is free, *and I'm not day-dreaming,*
whenever I look through my window.

MY HEART IS A VOLCANO

My heart is a volcano,
A cyclone, a shooting star,
My heart is a speeding freight train,
A runaway racing car.

My heart is a hunting cheetah,
An eagle soaring above the sea,
My heart is a captive lovebird
That's suddenly been set free.

My heart is a trembling gazelle,
Grazing the African plain,
My heart is a sleeping baby,
My dad is home again.

THE SOLDIER

The soldier stands in the midday sun
and stares down the dusty road,
and the gun upon his shoulder
feels like a heavy load.

The soldier stands in the dusty road,
face twisted in agony,
for the mortal enemy he hunts
are members of his own family.

The soldier stands by the barbed-wire fence,
under a pitiless sky.
He thinks of the home he's left behind,
and a tear slips from his eye.

The soldier sits by the camp fire,
and his eyes are baffled when
his comrades joke, he doesn't understand.
This soldier's only ten.

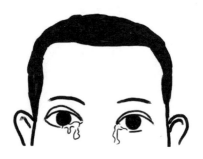

I OPENED THE DOOR
(AFTER WiLLiAM BLAKE)

I opened the door of my heart
And my enemy walked inside
He did not see the trap I'd set,
He walked straight in, and died.
I opened the door of my heart
Where my enemy met his end
And welcomed the one who walked out
Not my enemy but my friend.

RELIEF

When you're really, really coughing
And your throat is very sore,
When it aches if you start laughing
And if you talk it hurts some more,
When the sheets feel like sandpaper
As they rub against your skin,
When you wheeze and sneeze and shiver,
You feel weak and you look thin,
When Brazil and Argentina
Are playing football in your head,
When the thought of food upsets you
And you wish that you were dead,
When the sound of someone breathing
Is like thunder in your brain,
And the noise of a bee buzzing
Sounds just like an express train,

Then your brother gallops in,
Plops himself down on your bed,
He just misses the mattress
But he finds your legs instead,
And he bellows in your ear,
"What's the matter, are you ill?
Got a soaring temperature?
Have you caught a chill?"
Then he shoves his greasy burger
Right there underneath your nose,
And chomping on a mouthful,

"You don't want some, I suppose?"
You shout aloud for help,
But it's just a feeble croak,
And your brother starts to giggle,
And you wonder where's the joke.

But then your mother comes in
Just in time to rescue you,
And she shoos him out and tells him,
"Go and find something to do!"
Then she straightens up the pillows,
Smoothes the creases from the sheets,
Cools your head with a wet flannel,
With a smile that's warm and sweet.
And she places a soft kiss
In the middle of your brow,
And you wonder how it's happened
That you're feeling better now,
And she's reading you a story
In a soft and mellow voice,
It's the story you'd have chosen
If you could have made the choice,
And as you're drifting off to sleep,
A smile upon your face,
You think that life is good
And this world's a lovely place.

THE EYE

Watching, watching, watching, watching, watching

It's watching you, it's watching you,
Every move you make, the eye is watching you,
No matter where you go and no matter what you do,
It's recorded by that great eye, watching you.

Watching, watching, watching, watching, watching

You can't be liberated, there is no rescue
And you'll never for one minute be outside its view,
It knows your hopes and dreams, knows your secrets too,
Every thought you have that eye can see right through.

Watching, watching, watching, watching, watching

There's no need to feel distressed, no need for feeling blue,
No need to get excited or to misconstrue
Its actions, they're not meant to frighten or subdue,
For that giant watching eye, it belongs to you.

THE WALL

I'm building a wall
To keep you out
A wall of silence
Won't open my mouth
Won't say a word
Won't heave a sigh
Won't touch your hand
Won't catch your eye
I'm building a wall
A wall of hate
But I'll leave a gap
For a little gate.

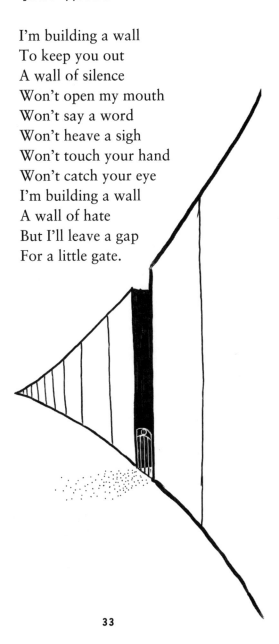

FUN
WITH
FORMS

TERMS

The SLAM of the door,
the STAMP on the floor,
is onomatopoeia.

When school bells CHIME
right on TIME,
that's rhyme.

If the boy IS AS FREE
AS a bird in a tree,
that's a simile.

When THE PUG SMILES at the dalmatian,
the WIND SINGS in exultation,
that's personification.

When the window's smashed to rubble,
Dad says, "Come here! At the double!"
That's trouble.

JOURNEY

What should I do for excitement and adventure?
Venture
And shall I dare, come sun or sleet or snow?
No!
Is that because the outcome is unsure?
Sure
Where should I avoid as I travel hill and valley?
Alley
Where can I find a certain source of pleasure?
Leisure
And where's the best place to find true diversity?
City
Will I succeed the harder that I try?
Aye
I'm worried that I'll try and fail, you know.
Oh!
What do I get if I should fail and try again?
A gain
How will I make friends when I hate conversing?

Sing
What if I find I'm not up to the task?
Ask
After that what's left me to enjoy?
Joy

GREEN

Green
The face
On the ship
Are you feeling OK?
Seasick.

CINQUAIN

AT ONCE

At once
From the mist of
Daybreak, a shadow looms,
A gate creaks and empty bottles
Clatter.

BEHiND A WHiTE WALL

A soldier I am
Trapped behind a white wall
I'm free to get out
Yet I can't escape at all.

TWiNS

We two are the shining twins,
We do everything together,
We are always side by side
In every kind of weather,
We sparkle like lamps all day long,
But when the darkness falls
We are two shrinking violets,
And we won't answer to your call.

Ten Sisters

We are ten sisters travelling together,
We are five pairs of identical twins,
We often make music and chatter together,
We don't go near creatures with wings, hooves or fins.
When the fat ones stand upright, it means everything's
OK,
But when they do a somersault, they have nothing
good to say.

The Pearl

A pearl I am, as white as snow,
Inside I keep a store of gold
Around which crystal waters flow,
Yet I don't fetch much when I am sold.

➞ If you'd like to check your answers go to p.96

YOU MADE ME TODAY

You made me today but I was made long ago
I work best when you're asleep
I'm something you won't give away
And yet don't wish to keep.

I've head one end and foot one end
But no body in between
Plants like roses have me
But not the kale or bean.

I have post but don't have letters
I wear clothes but don't wear shoes
If you're too fond of my company
You'll get sores, but not one bruise.

You'll lie when you are with me,
Though what you say is true
I'm busiest when you're idle
Though there's nothing I can do.

Though I'm always on your side
To love me too much is not right
I'll not pass the time of day with you
But I'll wish you a good night.

→ If you'd like to check your answer go to p.96

RONDEL

SORROW CALLED

Sorrow called while I was sleeping,
As he had done once before,
Prying open eyes still sore
From the endless bouts of weeping.

Scattering courage I'd been keeping
For a rainy day, in store,
Sorrow called while I was sleeping,
As he had done once before.

He walked not boldly, but came creeping
Like those robbers I abhor,
Came to wreck my life once more,
Bringing changes harsh and sweeping.
Sorrow called while I was sleeping.

NUMBERS

The numbers decided to dine,
The meal was going just fine,
But 6, 5 and 4
Headed straight for the door
When they saw that 789.

A Babysitter who Lived in Nantucket

A babysitter who lived in Nantucket,
Put the crying child in her pocket,
Her friend said, "Don't fret,
Sure the child is upset,
But that's an astronaut's baby, just rocket."

I Looked Into the Garden Shed

I looked into the garden shed
Before I could avert my gaze,
I wished that I had stayed in bed,
The sight would haunt my mind for days.
The sight would haunt my mind for days.
I wished that I had stayed in bed,
Before I could avert my gaze,
I looked into the garden shed.

SKELTONIC VERSE

Is verse that's terse
With rhyming words
Like birds and herds
Like curds and girds
And surds and thirds
Keep words going
And lines flowing
Till the rhymes you seek
Become quite weak
Then change the rhyme,
You'll see in time
They'll cease to chime
And that is when
You switch again.

Lines are stressed twice
(sometimes thrice)
And it's your choice
Either short and sweet
With a pronounced beat
Or make it long
With rhythm strong
Like a lilting song
Try writing one
You'll have such fun!

OUR WORLD

THE WEATHER'S BALL

Tornado tangoed with Thunder,
Lightning limboed with rain,
Hailstone partnered Blizzard,
Gale high-stepped with Hurricane.
Fog went to the ball with Drizzle,
Snow with her best friend Sleet,
Wind waltzed away with Cyclone,
Sunshine shimmied in with Heat.
Storm took to the floor with Warm Front,
Monsoon was led by Drought,
Tsunami came in with a huge fanfare,
Flashflood came in without.
Typhoon and Twister both arrived
with Tidal Wave and Squall,
but dressed in a dazzling rainbow,
young Cloud eclipsed them all.

THE MOON TOLD THE WIND

The moon told the wind
and the wind told the sea,
the sea told the trees
and the trees told me.

What they said was so exciting!
So amazing! And so true!
But they said it was a secret.
I'm so sorry, I can't tell you.

This Would Be Perfect

This would be perfect,
an idyll, a dream,
the song of the ocean,
the lullaby of the stream,
the sand like white crystals,
beneath the palm trees,
the sun kissing my shoulders,
the soft breath of the breeze.

This would be perfect,
lying here on the sunbed,
if I wasn't scared a coconut
might fall on my head.

ECLiPSE

A huge space giant saw the sun,
he thought it was a currant bun,
so he took an enormous bite
and turned the daytime into night.

VOLCANO

Don't go to look when it erupts,
fly in the opposite direction,
its molten rocks are always apt
to cause severe affliction.

Do not try to go potholing
deep inside its crater,
don't stand on top to peer inside,
the danger could not be greater.

Don't plant potatoes on its slope,
forget its fertile soil,
it's been programmed only to cause
destruction and turmoil.

Do not try to cook an egg
in its bubbling pool,
that's an action that's not taken
by smart people, as a rule.

Whatever you do, do not stand still
to watch its lava flow,
just heed the warning in its name,
it's called a volca... NO!

DAWN

Sunlight pries open
the hands of the mimosa
which all night had been clasped
in prayer.

INDiGESTiON

First there is a little grumble,
Then a loud and powerful rumble,
The mountain's got a dreadful bellyache,
It is shivering and it's shaking,
In its agony it's quaking
And its body is vibrating fit to break.

Then it swells up and it stretches
And suddenly it retches,
Spewing jets of fire high into the air,
Streams of magma, molten lava,
Like a skilful master carver
Etching patterns in the land like a ploughshare.

Then like a babe sucking its dummy,
When the fire in its tummy
Is ejected, it calmly goes to sleep.
It's now free from indigestion
And there's just a small suggestion
Of a soft contented sigh from way down deep.

THE SEA IS A WILD HORSE

The sea is a wild horse,
Rearing against the rocks
And trampling castles in the sand.

The castles are dreams
Of children, laughing with abandon,
Dancing among the boulders on the shore.

The children are messages
Tossed in bottles
Upon the turbulent sea of life.

The sea is a wild horse,
Rearing against the rocks
And trampling castles in the sand.

ORCHARD

I've planted a mango, a peach and a pear,
I'm growing an orchard right over there,
I'll be picking fruit any day now, I dare say,
For I planted the seeds early yesterday.

FOREST

Here at the edge, night shakes hands with day,
dark and light fused to a soft pastel grey.
Silent as a shadow's breath, the ceaseless snowflakes fall,
nothing living moves, no mousing owl's shrill call
disturbs the peace of winter, but the sentinel trees
shiver as they listen to the whispering breeze.
No straying footsteps have touched the settled snow,
no signposts point the travellers the way that they should go,
but there for the ones who are willing to see,
is a path that will lead them to a distant country,
and for the ones who are eager and willing to hear,
there's the sound of laughter and a welcoming cheer,
and voices are calling, "Where have you been?
We've been waiting for you. Come in, come in!"

ANIMALS

THE MOST DANGEROUS ANIMAL IN THE WORLD

The most dangerous animal in the world
is not the cobra with its hood unfurled,
not the bear, black, brown or grizzly,
Komodo with lethal saliva drizzly.

You'd think the black mamba with flickering tongue
would be most deadly, you'd be wrong.
It's not the horn of the bad-tempered rhino
you should fear most, nor the tiger's eye, no!

Not the lazy gaze or the cunning smile
of the salt-water crocodile.
The elephant could flatten you in a fight,
the hippo could kill you just with one bite.

But much more dangerous than these
is the tiny mosquito called *anopheles*,
who roams the world from Greenland to Australia,
and kills millions with malaria.

She's worse than those with vicious claws,
those who'll crush you in their jaws.
Luckily she's the only one who
you can squash before she bites you.

PiRANHA

We hide in the water
In the shadows beneath
As the sun's rays grow shorter
We hide in the water
Here's a man and his daughter
We avoid their flat feet
We hide in the water
In the shadows beneath.

RiVER DOLPHiN'S SONG

Among prawns, fish and frogs
That's where I like to be
In rivers and bogs
Among prawns, fish and frogs
Poking under stones and logs
Leaping high and swimming free
Among prawns, fish and frogs
That's where I like to be.

THE HUNT

She tried again with patience
to explain to him her sport,
he with his simple needs and
his simple mind (she thought).

"You take the net," she whispered.
"Try not to make a sound.
Walk slowly towards the creature,
and when it's settled on the ground

you bring the net down over it,
then remove it with your hand."
She waved the net before his face.
"Now do you understand?"

Still he shook his young head,
perplexity in his eyes.
"Why do you catch it?" he asked again.
"You can't eat butterflies."

POiSON DART FROG

He's a poison bottle,
He's a venom store,
In the jungles of South America,
In tree, on forest floor,
He's a champion archer,
And his poison dart
Is straight and true and deadly,
And he's aiming for your heart.
So when you're in the jungle
Under those infested trees,
And you feel an icy puff,
It may not be just a breeze.
You'd better wear some armour,
You'd better wear a hat,
For with one single little breath
He could knock you flat.
You'd better take a doctor,
You'd better take a nurse,
You'd better put some frog repellent
In your pocket or your purse.
Better pack some ammunition,
Some arrows and a bow,
In fact, I think it's best, Mum,
If you simply didn't go.

THE INLAND TAIPAN

It could kill a hundred men
with the venom in one bite,
it moves as fast as lightning
when it's got prey in its sight.

So I'm glad to find it's rather shy
and that if it had the choice,
though it could kill a hundred men,
it would rather feed on mice.

THE VULTURE

His eyes are sunken, bloodshot,
His neck scrawny and red,
He's only got himself to blame,
He will live off the dead.

PRAYING MANTIS

The praying mantis is not religious
Despite what you might hear,
Although it seems quite pious,
Its front legs clasped in prayer,
Before a meal, what it will say
Is not "Bless this food" but "Let us prey".

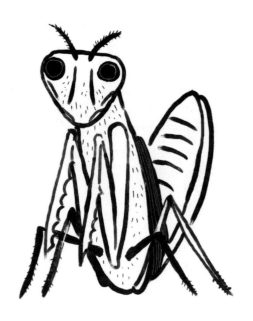

Roll Call

The Short-horned water buffalo
and the Western black rhino,

Small White-footed rabbit-rat,
Tanzanian woolly bat,

Sea mink, Corsican giant shrew,
Desert rat kangaroo,

Sturdees Bonin pipistrelle,
Queen of Sheba's or Yemen gazelle,

The quagga, the Atlantic grey whale,
and Canary Islands quail,

The Central hare-wallaby,
Dark flying-fox, Jamaican monkey,

The Giant ruffed and Sloth lemurs,
Sardinian Pika and hundreds more,

All amazing, all distinct,
and every one of them extinct.

MORE LINES ABOUT THE AUK

I hear some sailors found the auk,
When roasted, quite delectable,
And so they ate auk night and day,
Until the poor auk passed away,
Which I find unaukceptable.

TALENTED

The cricket's ears are in its legs,
the snake hears with its tongue,
the marsupial frog's back is lumpy and bumpy
because it is filled with her young.
The wrasse changes from mum to dad,
the clownfish from dad to mum,
the kangaroo has a pocket for her baby,
snug and warm, right next to her tum.
The fly on the plate seems to be dancing a jig
all over the veg and the meat,
the fly doesn't think it's attending a ball,
it's just that it tastes with its feet.
These animals are all quite clever,
at least from what I've read,
but I bet not a single one of them
can stand up on its head.

DON'T DO IT!
(FOR ETHAN)

Do not dress the llamas in pyjamas,
Do not put a shoe on the emu,
It's the height of foolishness
To put a rhino in a dress,
And they certainly won't thank you if you do.

Do not put a bracelet on the piglet,
Don't put a pinafore on the old boar,
And a hippo in a shirt
Will just wallow in the dirt
And you'll not be wearing that shirt any more.

Take that silly earring off the gosling,
Whoever heard of pants on elephants?
And high heels on a wild horse?
I can think of nothing worse,
It's preposterous and quite irrelevant.

Do not put a top hat on the meerkat,
Do not put that headgear on the deer,
Socks on lions are not smart,
They might bite you for a start,
And hyenas don't need ribbons in their hair.

Do not put those bloomers on the pumas,
Do not put a tutu on the gnu,
An arctic fox in a cagoule
Will just look and feel a fool,
And you'll no longer be a keeper in this zoo.

UNBELIEVABLE?

MY TEACHER PLAYS THE PiANO

My teacher plays the piano,
And long the music lingers,
He plays the piano by ear,
With lobes instead of fingers.

MY NOSE

My nose turned round to me one day
and said, *I want a break.*
I'm sick of whiffs and pongs;
there's just so much a nose can take.

I want to be eyes for a change
and look at pretty things
like lilacs, fishes, butterflies
and birdies on the wing.

That's not why you were made, I said.
You are not in a race.
Each of you in this body
has a different job and place.

I want to read love poetry,
said Nose, *to watch TV,*
I want to close up when I'm tired,
for a change eyes can be me.

So my nose that day became my eyes,
and while my eyes sniffed flowers,
my nostrils read the papers
and watched TV for hours.

It saw hurricanes in Mexico
and suffering in Iran.
It watched the fighting in Syria,
earthquakes in Pakistan.

It saw gun fights on New York streets
and floods in Bangladesh,
It read the stories of Beowulf,
Jason, and Gilgamesh.

My nose turned round to me and said,
OK, I've had enough,
I cannot understand how eyes
can take in all this stuff.

It's clear I was not made to see,
you're right, I can't compete.
I think I'd rather skip and jump,

so can I be your feet?

THE ISLE OF NEGATYVES

Do not come here without protection,
For on this isle is a large collection
Of monsters, all of different size,
From huge Kantdos with bulbous eyes

To the tiny Wunt with needle tongue,
Which likes to incubate its young
In the soft flesh behind your neck.
If you must come, be sure to check

You have strong ointment of Willdo,
For that's the only way that you
Will escape from the small Wunt's sting.
And be very sure to bring

A large bottle of Iamsure,
If not you will for evermore
Be wondering what is right, or wrong,
For the Maybee's poison's very strong.

And do not say you were not warned.
Here the sly misstrusts are spawned,
They'll burrow deep into your brain,
You'll never be the same again.

Bring certaynties, for they'll ward off
The incredulouse with its scornful laugh,
Or she'll fill your mind with tiny doughts.
Those little creatures' raucous shouts

Attract a host of mocking wurds,
And these sharply taloned birds
Will not cease from their fierce attack,
Until you're lying on your back

Without an ounce of dignity,
Pierced by their harsh malignity.
Mix certaynties with Iwontlissen,
A little pinch, your eyes will glisten

With confidence. This will scare
Those vicious wurds to Whoknowswhere.
And that's the best way to subdue
Those spiteful creatures who'd hurt you.

NAMES

There is no brim on the cap of my knee,
No keys for the locks in my hair,
I looked for the pearls in the crown of my head,
But didn't find a single one there.

My calves will not grow up to be cows,
You can't walk on the bridge of my nose,
Though I tried I could not make a box or a house
With the nails on the tips of my toes.

You won't get dates from the palms of my hands,
My pupils do not go to school,
No music will come from the drums in my ears,
Or treasure from my chest, as a rule.

There are no legs on the mole on my arm,
No fruits on the stem of my brain,
And no one worships in the temple on my head.
Who's in charge of this naming again?

STRANGE

There are two giant lobsters
Talking on the telephone,
An Alsatian is evolving
Out of a marrowbone.

A man is by the window
Sitting in a giant boot,
A preacher is giving a sermon
To a twisting oak tree root.

That woman in the swimming pool
Is riding on a whale,
A giant snake devours himself
Beginning at his tail.

Two dogs are chasing shadows
Outside an empty room,
A girl sits counting marbles
In a superman costume.

My one's the albino mouse
With a cheeseboard for a heart,
I can't wait for next week's classes,
It's such fun, this Modern Art.

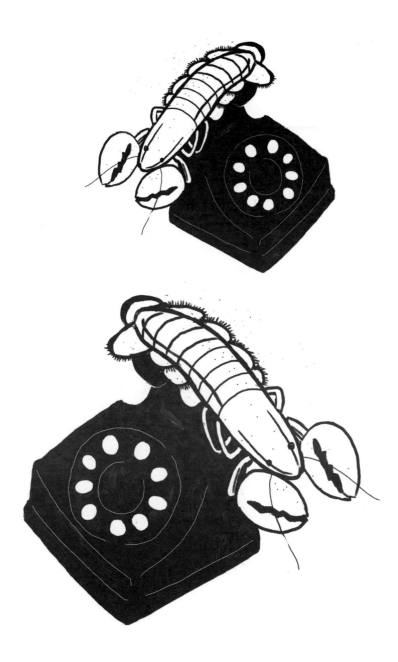

85

THE ZiMBATS

The Zimbats came from Zingley Dell,
Purple and orange and free,
Their hearts were in the right place,
But there was only a space where their brains should be.
Only a space where their brains should be.

They came in droves from the hills, they came,
Looking for something to eat,
Some fruit or veg if they could find,
Or a tasty piece of meat,
For in their land they'd nothing left,
Except one grain of wheat.

They climbed to the tops of banana trees,
Picked bananas hand by hand,
And their black tears fell like burning soot
Upon the pinky sand.
"These plants will wave no more," they said,
"Without each little hand."

The Zimbats came from Zingley Dell,
Purple and orange and free,
Their hearts were in the right place,
But there was only a space where their brains should be.
Only a space where their brains should be.

They raided a field of broccoli
Beside the waterfront,
 Each tucked into the broccoli spears
With a soft contented grunt.
"Without their spears," they wiped a tear,
"How will the broccoli hunt?"

They guzzled fried fish fingers,
Cut from cods and hakes and plaices,
And as they chomped, the bitter tears
Streamed down their purple faces.
"Poor little fish!" they cried, "for now
You cannot tie your laces."

The Zimbats came from Zingley Dell,
Purple and orange and free,
Their hearts were in the right place,
But there was only a space where their brains should be.
Only a space where their brains should be.

They foraged for some sugar cane
As they trumbled along,
They chewed the roots, the stems, the flags,
And mourned, "This is so wrong.
Without their flags, the canes won't know
To which country they belong."

They pounced on purple eggplants
Growing in an eggplant patch,
And they long and loud lamented
When they'd finished the last batch.
"Without its eggs, we cannot hope
This plant will ever hatch."

The Zimbats came from Zingley Dell,
Purple and orange and free,
Their hearts were in the right place,
But there was only a space where their brains should be.
Only a space
Only a space
Only a space
Where their brains should be.

JACK'S MOTHER

He was always being conned by some crook's money-
    making scheme.
He'd bought sweaters for fishes, wellies for frogs, a bike
    that ran on steam,
so I warned him when I sent him off to market with the
    cow,
"Don't you go and lose this one the way you lost the
    sow."

He didn't bring back ten pounds, not one, not fifty
    pence.
"Beans!" I yelled. "Five stupid beans! Boy, have you
    got no sense?"
I hurled them out the window, as far as I could throw,
but for once he wasn't lying; you should have seen those
    five beans grow!

Next thing he's climbing up to heaven, and then he's
    back with gold.
"Enough," I said after the hen, but he would not be
    told.
I was trying on my new dress when I heard him shout,
    "Mum, quick!
Bring the axe!" I looked up and I can tell you I felt sick.

But all's well, we're rich and happy (so I had to beg his
    pardon),
and he's charging folk a pound to see the dead giant in
    the garden.

THE SELLER

He walked through the streets, from door to door,
he called through the streets till his throat was sore.
"Come look at the treasures I have to sell,
cooling waters from a bottomless well,
ointment for your eyes, so you can see
everything clearly, for eternity.
Come eat of my bread, and you'll never die,
come out of your houses, come buy, come buy."

But they shook their heads and with mournful sigh
said, "We have no money with which to buy.
We would love to eat of your marvellous bread,
who'd choose to die if they could live instead?
Your wares are tempting, but we are poor,
we have no money, please go from our door."

"Do not fret about money," the seller replied.
"I don't need your pennies, so put them aside,
but I'll take instead the tears from your eyes,
give me your heartaches, your groans and your sighs.
Bring me your pain and your misery
and I'll give you fruit from a life-giving tree,
fruit that will keep you from growing old,
countless nuggets of purest gold,
garments woven from precious threads,
crowns studded with jewels to grace your heads."

But the people murmured, and the people frowned,
and soon the seller's words were drowned
by angry voices and furious shouts.
"Get rid of this man, go on, throw him out!
He's come here to mock us, to waste our time,
he's spreading lies and that's a crime,
who's ever heard of anything good,
clothes or vehicles or tools or food,
being bought without money, being sold without
     price?
He's holding us to ridicule, and that's not nice."

They banged their windows and slammed their
     doors,
they called him names, they cursed and swore,
they stopped their ears to his plaintive cries,
they did not see the tears in his eyes
as he went knocking from door to door
of apartment blocks, of high-rise floors.
"Why hunger and thirst? Why would you die?
Come buy my treasures, come buy! Come buy!"

The Colours of My Dreams

Once I held inside my palms
the curviness of a bow,
and listened in the cornfield
to the sadness of a scarecrow.

I clearly saw the saltiness
of the Atlantic Ocean,
watched a mother with her newborn babe
and tasted her devotion.

Once I heard the vibrant green
of a lawn that was just laid,
smelt the laughter of the children
playing in the glade,

I once heard the roundness
of a brand new tennis ball
and touched the despair of a man
with his back against the wall.

I travelled once around the world
on stars with flaming tails,
and touched the colours of my dreams
along some silver trails.

ABOUT THE POET AND THE iLLUSTRATOR

VALERiE BLOOM MBE is the author of several volumes of poetry for adults and children, picture books, pre-teen and teenage novels and stories for children, and has edited a number of collections of children's poetry. She has presented poetry programmes for the BBC, and has contributed to various radio and television programmes.

Her poetry has been featured in 'Poetry on the underground', and included in the GCSE and Caribbean exam syllabuses. Her poetry is also included in over 500 anthologies.

Valerie Bloom has been awarded an Honorary Masters Degree from the University of Kent, and an MBE from the queen for services to poetry. She lives in Kent and performs her poetry, runs writing workshops and conducts training courses for teachers worldwide. Books include *Let Me Touch the Sky*, *Hot Like Fire*, *Whoop an' Shout* and *Surprising Joy*.

KEN WiLSON-MAX was born in Zimbabwe and is an internationally renowned children's book illustrator, author and designer and co-director of publishing house Alanna Max. He wrote and illustrated *Astro Girl*, winner of the 2020 STEAM award. He lives in London.

➡ Answers p.40–41: Behind a White Wall (*tongue*), Twins (*eyes*), Ten Sisters (*fingers*), The Pearl (*an egg*); p.42: You Made Me Today (*bed*).